Anna's Song

Written and illustrated by Marty Baker

Collins

Anna loved to sing. Her singing was sweet and strong.

When Anna was little, Meena sang along with her. They were like sisters.

But as the years went by, the rest of
the children started to feel Anna didn't fit in.

They felt her constant singing was odd.
Meena stopped singing with Anna.

But Anna *had* to sing. When she felt flustered or stressed, she sang a lot. It was the one thing that helped her feel better.

The rest of the children didn't understand.
They complained that Anna sang too much.

Miss Sparks said, "Hush now, Anna. I need to explain this lesson."

It was hard for Anna to explain that singing was important.

Anna felt abandoned by them all. Her singing got fainter and fainter. She started to look sadder and sadder.

9

One morning, Anna stood singing by herself under a tree. All of a sudden, there was a faint honking and tweeting.

Anna spun to see what it was. It was Meena
– with her clarinet!

Meena said, "I feel bad that I stopped singing with you. Can I join in?"

Anna was so glad, she felt she was floating.

Little by little, things were less of a strain.
With Meena next to her, Anna started to
feel confident.

The rest of the children let them be.

When Anna sang and Meena joined in on the clarinet, they felt so strong.

Now, when Anna sings, her song rings out clear and free.

Anna's album

Meena's clarinet

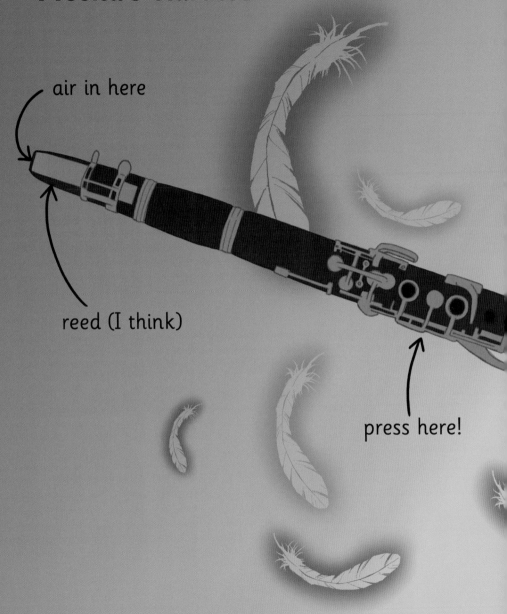

air in here

reed (I think)

press here!

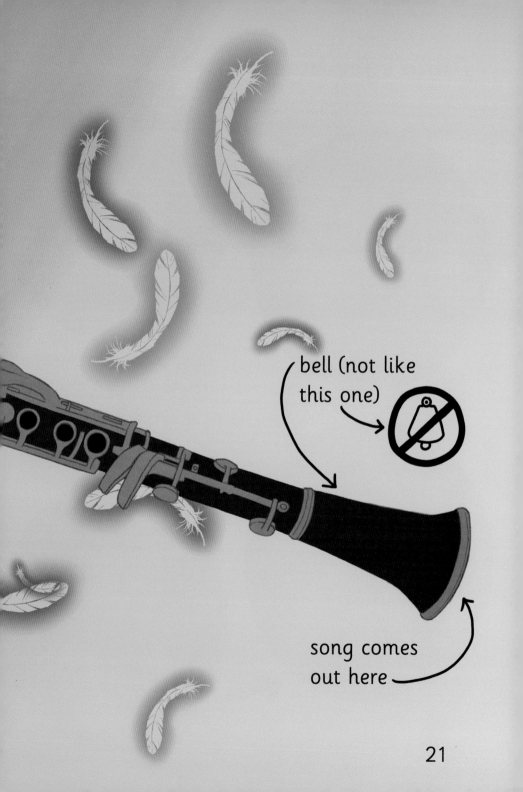

bell (not like this one)

song comes out here

Anna's feelings

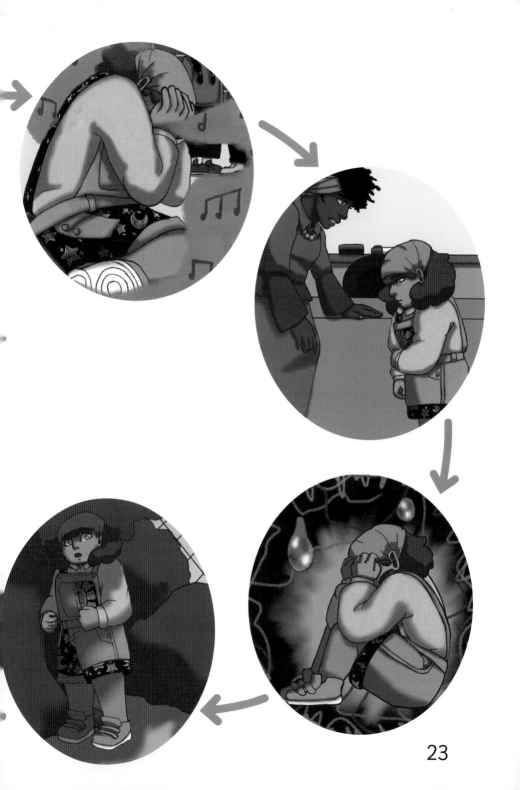

 Review: After reading

Use your assessment from hearing the children read to choose any GPCs, words or tricky words that need additional practice.

Read 1: Decoding

- Point to **abandoned** on page 9. Discuss its meaning (*left alone*). Ask the children whether this makes sense in the story – in what ways might Anna have felt left? (e.g. *Meena stopped singing with her; the children didn't show understanding; Miss Sparks didn't seem to understand*)

- Ask the children to read these words. Encourage them to sound them out in "chunks" or syllables if it helps:
  und/er/stand   com/plained   flust/ered   ex/plain   im/por/tant

- Challenge the children to take turns to read a page aloud, but sounding out words silently.

Read 2: Prosody

- Model reading pages 8 and 9, using tone and emphasis to dramatise.

- Ask the children to practise reading a page each with a partner. Can they be a good storyteller and draw the listener in?

- Encourage them to show the meaning of words through the way they say them, for example getting fainter as they read **fainter and fainter**.

Read 3: Comprehension

- Ask the children how singing or listening to music makes them feel. Does it make them feel happy or sad? Why?

- Look together at the back-cover blurb. Ask the children why they think the author chose to write this story. What does it teach us? (e.g. *to try to understand people and be kind*) What could Anna's classmates have done to make Anna feel more included?

- Turn to pages 22 and 23. Challenge the children to retell the story in role as Meena. What happens at each stage of the story and how does she feel?

- Bonus content: Ask the children to read pages 20 and 21, then describe how they think the clarinet works.

- Bonus content: Encourage the children to come up with the start, middle and end of a new story about Meena and Anna, using the pictures on pages 18 and 19 for ideas.
  - Discuss what event or setting might get Anna **flustered** or **stressed**.
  - What will the rest of the children do? Will they show understanding now? What will Anna do to help Meena?

To find out more about this book and the author go to: collins.co.uk/BooksLikeMe